WHAT TO SAY WHEN

She's Not Sure She Believes in God Anymore

BRIANNA REEVES

Library of Congress Cataloging-in-Publication Data

Names: Reeves, Brianna, author.
Title: What to say when she's not sure she believes in God anymore / Brianna Reeves.
Description: Phillipsburg, New Jersey : P&R, [2025] | Summary: "When someone expresses doubts about her faith, how do you respond? Reeves helps readers to listen to another's doubts with solemnity, curiosity, and hope-then engage in wise and practical ways"-- Provided by publisher.
Identifiers: LCCN 2025002019 | ISBN 9798887791395 (paperback) | ISBN 9798887791401 (epub)
Subjects: LCSH: Belief and doubt. | Belief and doubt--Biblical teaching. | Faith--Christianity. | Faith--Biblical teaching.
Classification: LCC BT774 .R448 2025 | DDC 234/.23--dc23/eng/20250215
LC record available at https://lccn.loc.gov/2025002019

So, she's said it. Maybe you suspected this was coming, or maybe it's a complete shock.

"I'm not sure if I believe in God anymore."

Walking with someone through doubt or deconstruction can be daunting. There's a lot at stake. What if you say the wrong thing? What if you can't answer her questions? What if her doubts cause you to doubt? But the truth is that doubt does not spell the end of Christian faith, and God can use this experience powerfully in both your friend's life and yours. This resource is designed to help you counsel a doubting friend with compassion, curiosity, and hope.

In my own seasons of doubt, wise women have held on to me gently and firmly. They have upheld me in prayer. They have held my fears and unspeakable questions. They have held my hand and walked with me through dark nights and valleys of shadow (Ps. 23). My hope is that you and I would learn to be companions like these.

Perhaps she is a dear friend—someone you have served with, prayed with, and laughed with for years. She might be someone you formally mentor—a member of your youth group or Bible study. Or maybe you don't know her well at all. Whoever she is, for the purposes of this book, we're going to call her Jen.

It's possible that you've noticed that Jen has been acting strangely. She seems distant, resistant, or somehow sensitive. Perhaps she's found excuses to miss church recently or has stepped back from a ministry position. Or perhaps you haven't noticed anything awry. She seems like her usual self—in fact, just last week she was offering insightful answers at your Bible study.

Either way, Jen asks to speak to you. As your conversation unfurls, a knot forms in your stomach. You can tell she is nervous. She's been feeling like this for a long time, she says. She still wants to be friends. She thinks she'll take some time away from church, to figure things out. She blinks back tears.

Jen isn't sure she believes in God anymore.

This is a difficult confession to hear. You might feel shocked. You might feel anxious for Jen, worried about her spiritual well-being and future. You might even feel angry or betrayed, especially if she is a church leader or a close friend. Relationships in the church are unique: Jen is (or was?) your sister. You thought you were on the same page. Suddenly the rules of the game have changed, and you can't help but wonder,

- Is our friendship over?
- Can I help her, or is it too late?
- What is going to happen to her?

- If I try to change her mind, will I push her further away?
- Was she ever a Christian at all?
- Do I need to tell someone else about this?

Before we go any further, however, I want you to take a step back and put yourself in Jen's shoes. Something has led her to this point. She is suffering; the turmoil of doubt is acutely painful . . . in fact, it's the most painful thing I myself have ever experienced. Jen likely feels disconnected from her friends, her community, and even herself. She may be disillusioned, confused, and completely alone. For months or years, she has been kept awake by unanswerable questions. She has lost something precious, and she's just been brave enough to tell you. She has let you into her suffering.

This is a privilege. Jen trusts you enough to share this burden with you. She is willing to be honest and vulnerable. Her confession is a small signal fire of hope . . . of faith, even. When a man confessed his doubt to Jesus and cried, "Help my unbelief," Jesus honored his request (Mark 9:24 ESV). The Lord holds doubters safe in his hands. Take courage, friend, and thank God for giving you the privilege of walking alongside your sister through her suffering.

The Heart of the Struggle

Doubt is not one-size-fits-all. When Jen says, "I'm not sure if I believe in God anymore," she could mean a few different things. She may mean that she doubts God's existence, or she may mean that she no longer feels his presence. She may mean that she feels deeply disappointed in God and no longer trusts that he is good or sovereign. She may have made a firm decision not to believe in God, or she may feel herself to be slowly drifting toward unbelief.

Your priority is to keep open the lines of communication between you and Jen. James 1:19 counsels us to "be quick to listen, slow to speak." So, before you say anything, start by listening. Don't interrupt Jen, and don't make assumptions. Before you are able to offer any counsel or insight, you need to listen to, and understand, what Jen herself is going through.

Doubt encompasses a very broad spectrum of experiences. So too does faith. The Bible's definition of faith is multifaceted—it is not a formula. Enriching your own definition of faith will help you make space to understand Jen's complex experiences. When the time comes for you to speak, your definition of faith will help her see that there is another path. The thing she fears she may have lost may be closer than she knows.

The Heart of Faith

Faith is a gift. In Ephesians 2:8, Paul describes faith as "the gift of God." Only the Holy Spirit can give someone the ability to see Jesus for who he is, and only by the work of the Holy Spirit will anyone desire to surrender to him: "No one can say, 'Jesus is Lord,' except by the Holy Spirit"

(1 Cor. 12:3). This truth is what sits behind the New Testament's rich metaphor of spiritual blindness (Mark 8:22–25; Luke 24:30–32; Acts 9:18). No one can muster up their own faith. It is given by God.

Faith is an allegiance. In his seminal book on the Christian faith, *Mere Christianity*, C. S. Lewis writes, "Faith . . . is the art of holding on to things your reason has once accepted, in spite of your changing moods."* Feelings come and go, but faith is an act of the will. This is why God can "command" us to "believe in the name of his Son" (1 John 3:23). It does not make any sense to command someone to have a feeling. You can, however, command someone to make a decision. In keeping with the idea of faith as allegiance, the Bible uses military language to describe a Christian's determined commitment to Jesus, come what may:

> Stand firm then, with the belt of truth buckled around your waist, with the breastplate of righteousness in place, and with your feet fitted with the readiness that comes from the gospel of peace. (Eph. 6:14–15)

Faith is rational. Christianity has a long and rich history of intellectual rigor. Christians are thinking people and have been at the forefront of much academic and social progress. The Bible is a historical document that posits

---

* C. S. Lewis, *Mere Christianity* (repr., Macmillan, 1952), 109.

both theological and historical truths that are open to investigation. Luke's gospel begins with a clear statement of both intent and genre: "With this in mind, since I myself have carefully investigated everything from the beginning, I too decided to write an orderly account" (Luke 1:3). Many, many people have followed in Luke's footsteps, investigating the claims of the Bible and finding them to be both compelling and trustworthy. For some, this kind of study will greatly encourage their faith.

Faith is childlike trust. While the Christian faith is rational, it requires more than head knowledge. In fact, Jesus says the people who know the least often know the most. In Matthew 18:3, he praises children's innocent trust as a model of faith. Children do not have all the answers. They are not composed or calculating—and they are not always brave either. Having the faith of a child means trusting God because of who you know him to be . . . in spite of everything you don't know.

Faith is action. Faith does not live in our heads alone—or even in our hearts. Christian faith expresses itself in a life lived in a particular direction: the direction of Christlikeness. James 2:14–26 says that faith without action is "dead" (v. 17). Action is not only evidence of faith; it is faith itself. Read through the Sermon on the Mount in Matthew 5–7 and count how many times Jesus commanded his followers to *do* something. Obeying those commands is not separate from faith; it is a demonstration of faith. Faith means following Jesus. It is an activity.

Faith is clinging on to God. Sometimes faith is simply a desperate cry for help. It is lament. It is taking your anxieties somewhere—to someone. "Out of the depths I cry to you, LORD" (Ps. 130:1). King David, a man after God's own heart, wrote dozens of psalms of lament. He was desperately confused at times. Scared. Angry. He wrote about feeling abandoned by God. Yet Jews and Christians alike praise him as a man of great faith. When things just don't make sense, faith responds by simply clinging on.

As you listen to Jen, pay attention to whether her current definition of faith is broad or narrow. Does she resonate with any of the reflections above? Her understanding of faith may give you some helpful points for discussion.

Jen's Heart

When you talk to Jen about her experience of doubt, gently use the questions below to deepen your understanding of her story and of what is going on in her heart. The paragraphs that follow provide guidance for responding to possible answers that she might give.

- What is it about God that you're struggling to believe?

- How do you feel about this?
- How did you arrive in this place?
- Are you experiencing doubt more as a feeling or as a decision?
- Have you told anyone about this?
- What do you want your relationship with church to look like now?
- What aspects of the Christian faith still resonate with you?

If Jen feels good about her journey of deconstruction. Sometimes people feel a sense of freedom or relief during or after deconversion. I have found this to be relatively rare for people who once genuinely identified as Christian, but it does happen. If this is how Jen feels, you might want to ask more about her previous experience of Christian faith and community.

Has she been part of an unhealthy spiritual environment or been subject to unbiblical teaching? Often the shackles that people are keen to escape aren't shaped by sound Christian belief at all. Tragically, in the name of Christianity, Jen might have experienced sexism, racism, favoritism, or authoritarian church leadership. She might be rebelling against an unhealthy or alienating Christian culture rather than against the Christian faith itself. If this is the case, it's crucial for you to empathize with and affirm her concerns. Jen may not recognize the distinction between Christian culture, distortions of Christianity, and Christianity itself, so this could be a good opportunity for you to open the Scriptures together, if she is willing, and explore real Christianity.

Sometimes, though, people feel good about deconstructing because it offers them newfound "freedom." All of us want to live life according to our rules, and we're tempted to think that walking away from religion will give us the autonomy we crave. Indeed, the Bible teaches that sin is "lawlessness" (1 John 3:4)—it happens when we go our own way out of a stubborn belief that we know better than God. Jen might be feeling good about deconstructing because going our own way does feel good for a time—exhilarating, even—and, as you speak to her, you should keep in mind the ways that you give in to this same temptation. Yet the Bible, and even common sense, tell us that following our own intuitions and desires is not always wise. If you have the relational currency with Jen to be able to say so honestly, you can begin to explain this gently and slowly, after you have done the important work of listening.

If Jen feels distressed by her experiences of doubt. Most of the time, doubt is accompanied by anxiety, guilt, and even depression. Deconstruction is exactly what it sounds like—it involves taking apart the structures of one's life, bit by bit. A loss of faith also comes with a loss of relationships, roles, and a sense of purpose and direction. This is often painful and scary, and if Jen is dismayed or upset, your first role is to care for her. If she needs to cry, let her. Such grief is a healthy and necessary response to doubt. Her distress demonstrates a lingering love for God, his ways, and his people. Take comfort in this and, when the time is right, encourage Jen to take comfort in it too.

If Jen has big questions about God's existence or the Christian doctrine of God. Depending on your own level of knowledge, you might want to equip yourself with some reliable apologetics and theology resources as you seek to respond to Jen. Even if her questions overwhelm you, try not to run from them. Trust that someone can help you give her a defensible answer. It is good to demonstrate to Jen that the Christian faith is rational and that Christians are willing to engage humbly in robust discussion.

You don't have to be an expert. Don't be afraid to tell her, "I don't know how to answer that question, but let's find out together." Honesty can be profoundly encouraging for someone who is wrestling with doubt. If you acknowledge that you don't have all the answers, Jen will see that she doesn't need to either. Faith isn't synonymous with certainty, and questions—even very difficult ones—are a normal part of the Christian walk. Your friendship with Jen can become a safe place for you both to explore them.*

---

* Some helpful resources to start with are Timothy Keller, *The Reason for God* (repr., Penguin Books, 2018); Lee Strobel,

It is worth keeping in mind that even the most intellectual doubts are often rooted in feeling. There may well be something else, something more emotional, lurking behind Jen's questions. Perhaps she has experienced the pain of church conflict or even spiritual abuse. Perhaps she feels profoundly disappointed by the moral failures of Christian leaders. Grief, anxiety, and depression can all lead to existential doubt. We will explore those issues shortly. For now, as you explore her doubts, keep an ear out for her heart—for that always lies at the root of doubt.

There may also come a time when reading and research stop being helpful. Although this kind of study is helpful to a point, it has no real end. Finite minds can simply never grasp all there is to know about an infinite God. The Christian worldview can provide satisfying answers, but faith is more than a research project—it's not merely intellectual; it's also experiential and embodied. Particularly for chronic doubters, research can become an emotional Band-Aid or an obsession that draws them into an unhealthy spiral down the rabbit hole of internet apologists. Be discerning as you share resources with Jen and model a balanced approach. Sleep, exercise, and

---

The Case for Christ, updated ed. (Zondervan, 2016); Kevin DeYoung, *Taking God at His Word* (Crossway, 2014); Rebecca McLaughlin, *Confronting Christianity* (Crossway, 2019); Francis A. Schaeffer, *The God Who Is There* (Inter-Varsity Press, 1968); as well as Lewis, *Mere Christianity* (cited earlier).

laughter with friends are equally important medicine for those who are spiritually suffering.

If Jen's experience of God or of the Christian faith has changed. Sometimes doubt is less intellectual or emotional and more experiential. Perhaps Jen is struggling to understand whether God has changed or she has. *Has God abandoned me? Did I just imagine my previous spiritual experiences?* If Jen is asking these questions, you'll find it worthwhile to dig a little deeper into her expectations for the Christian life.

It is helpful to acknowledge the spectrum of normal Christian experiences. Some believers feel an intense connection with God, and others have a more rational and perhaps "dry" faith. It's even common for both experiences to fluctuate and evolve across a single believer's lifetime. The Bible's criteria for being a Christian do not revolve around the degree to which someone experiences God (whatever that even means!). No, Scripture is clear that "if you declare with your mouth, 'Jesus is Lord,' and believe in your heart that God raised him from the dead, you will be saved" (Rom. 10:9).

Despite this, many Christian traditions set us up to expect consistently profound emotional religious experiences. I don't think a study of Scripture or Christian history would lead us to this expectation. For thousands of years, believers have been writing about their experience of "the dark night of the soul," which is a season of spiritual dryness or emptiness. Twentieth-century preacher Martyn Lloyd-Jones referred to this as "spiritual depression." God's goodness and presence do not rely on our experience of him, and although it is undoubtedly painful when he seems to withdraw from us, this is a relatively normal part of the Christian life.

The Westminster Confession of Faith, written almost four hundred years ago, also speaks to this experience. Section 18.4 says that many things may well "shake" or "diminish" the assurance of "true believers." If we are "negligen[t] in preserving" our faith, or if we fall into "some special sin, which woundeth the conscience," or into "sudden or vehement temptation," our faith may suffer. The Confession also acknowledges the influence of factors outside our control, such as suffering and "God's withdrawing the light of his countenance."

Importantly, although it says we can expect such things to happen, the Confession reassures us that God will never abandon his people. Their doubt will lift, and their assurance will be restored: "Yet are they never utterly destitute of that seed of God, and life of faith, that love of Christ and the brethren, that sincerity of heart and conscience of duty, out of which, by the operation of the Spirit, this assurance may in due time be revived, and by the which, in the meantime, they are supported from utter despair." God, in his goodness, can work even an experience like Jen's for the "good of those who love him" (Rom. 8:28). In my own life, I have seen God use struggles with doubt to humble me and deepen my dependence on him.

If Jen is struggling to believe that God is good or if she has experienced significant suffering. This is a unique kind of doubt—and it deserves to be treated as such. Such doubt naturally arises from a broken or weary heart. It has significant biblical precedent: The book of Job, King David's psalms, and even Jesus's own prayer life affirm a response to suffering that consists of the cry "My God, my God, why have you forsaken me?" It is right for us to mourn the brokenness of life and to long for God's healing presence.

Doubts of this kind may slowly dissipate as a season of suffering lifts. Attending to Jen's suffering may therefore relieve her experience of doubt. Take care of her the same way you would care for anyone going through a hard season. Be present in her life to offer her companionship and even healthy distraction. Facilitate access to a trusted family doctor, counselor, or psychologist. Your support is essential to Jen's spiritual well-being, but there may be issues that are "above your pay grade," so to speak. Doubt and mental health are intertwined, and Jen may need to access professional help—for her sake and yours.

That doesn't mean your role becomes redundant. No matter her circumstances, she needs the practical care of a friend. Take her out for lunch. Organize a meal roster for her. Clean her house or organize babysitting. I don't know what kind of suffering sits behind Jen's doubts—

but hopefully at this point, you do. Use your God-given wisdom to serve as a sister for Jen, showing her the very love of God.

There may be underlying theological issues to discuss too. Unsound theology, such as the so-called "prosperity gospel," can set people up for profound hurt. If Jen has been taught to expect a life of abundance, then you will need to begin to slowly unwind this shiny but deceptive promise. Suffering often brings up important questions about the nature of evil and God's sovereignty, so equip yourself to answer these questions, or else refer Jen to someone who can. This book doesn't have room to address issues like this in detail, but here are some scriptural principles you can explore in your own time:

- In this life, we will all experience suffering (Gen. 3:16–19).
- Sin is the cause of suffering, but our suffering does not always result from our *own* sin. The whole of creation is impacted by sin, and we will feel the terrible effects of this sometimes (Rom. 8:22).
- Christians can expect to experience a particular kind of suffering because of our faith (1 Peter 4:12–13).
- When we suffer in this way, we are emulating Christ's suffering (Luke 14:27; Phil. 3:10).
- God uses our suffering to form our character (Rom. 5:3–4).

- Jesus conquered sin on the cross and will abolish all suffering when he returns (Rom. 8:18; Rev. 21:4).

Many excellent resources are available to help you unpack these important and complex ideas.*

If Jen has experienced spiritual abuse or church conflict. Spiritual abuse is when someone—often a religious leader, parent, or partner—uses religious beliefs to harm, scare, or control another person. Doubt about the character or provision of God is a natural and understandable response. And while serious church conflict may not involve spiritual abuse, it can result in similar feelings of betrayal and suspicion.

If Jen has gone through either of these experiences, you might want to direct her to passages from Jesus and Paul that outline the high calling of the church. God very clearly requires Christian leaders to practice justice, kindness, and gentleness, and he condemns any who fail to live up to his standards (Matt. 7:15; James 3:1). Affirm the anger and hurt she likely feels and reassure her that those who mistreated her were not reflecting God's character. After this, your response should follow the

---

* A couple to start with are Paul David Tripp, *Suffering* (Crossway, 2018), and Amy Orr-Ewing, *Where Is God in All the Suffering?* (The Good Book Company, 2020).

principles laid out in the section on suffering on pages 16–18.* Lord willing, Jen will come to distinguish Jesus's righteous ways from the callousness or cruelty she has experienced at the hands of so-called Christians.

Don't Throw the Baby Out with the Bathwater

There is one question I would particularly encourage you to ask Jen: *What aspects of the Christian faith still resonate with you?* This question can be revolutionary for doubters. Jen probably feels as if she is standing at the precipice of a life-changing identity crisis. Common narratives surrounding doubt force people into a binary approach to faith: It's all or nothing. You can offer Jen the opportunity to hold on to something that she loves. When she does this, her door to Christian faith remains open, and she is free to stand by the doorway for a while rather than feeling as if she must turn her back and leave. If she has anything positive to say about Christianity, lean into those things that still resonate with her.

A dear friend of mine, then in the process of deconstruction, said to me, "I don't want to throw the baby out with the bathwater." There were things about her Christian faith that she wanted to hold on to. Over time, her

---

* For a short introduction to trauma and a trauma-informed response, see Darby A. Strickland, *Trauma: Caring for Survivors* (P&R Publishing, 2023).

list grew; she held on to more and more. Importantly, she held on to Jesus—and, even more importantly, he held on to her. Jesus said of his disciples, "No one will snatch them out of my hand" (John 10:28). This is a precious promise, and one that I've seen come true over and over. Although I am still waiting to see the fulfillment of this promise in the lives of some I know, I have seen enough, and experienced enough in my own life, to take Jesus at his word when he says his grip is strong.

If Jen resonates with the concept of God's love, use this as an inroad to encourage her. If she still thinks the Bible has wisdom to offer, read it with her. If she enjoys Christian community, encourage her to invest in her relationships with believers. If she still finds herself drawn to the person of Jesus, speak about your personal relationship with him and ask questions about her impressions of him. If she still believes in life after death and ultimate meaning, direct the conversation to those topics. Each of these can serve as entry points for a conversation about the gospel—and the Savior—Jen needs.

Good News for Doubters

What does the gospel have to say about doubt? Fortunately, Jesus's lordship is good news that brings hope to the burdened and confused. What Jen needs most, more than any other wisdom you can offer her, is the gospel.

The Christian Faith Isn't for the Strong or Certain

Christianity is for the weak. In fact, it is only when we know our need that we can accept what Jesus offers. Jesus says, "It is not the healthy who need a doctor, but the sick. I have not come to call the righteous, but sinners" (Mark 2:17). God is not threatened by Jen's questions. Her doubts do not disqualify her from having a relationship with him because her relationship with God has never been contingent on her. None of us can stand before God on our own merit. It is not the strength of our faith that saves us; it is the strength of our Savior. This is why Paul warns the Roman church, "Do not think of yourself more highly than you ought, but rather think of yourself with sober judgment, in accordance with the faith God has distributed to each of you" (Rom. 12:3).

There are plenty of doubters in the Bible. Over and over, we see that God had compassion for them and invited them to trust his promise "My grace is sufficient for you, for my power is made perfect in weakness" (2 Cor. 12:9). In a lament filled with doubt and confusion, David pleaded,

> How long, LORD? Will you forget me forever?
>> How long will you hide your face from me?
>> How long must I wrestle with my thoughts
>>> and day after day have sorrow in my heart?
>> How long will my enemy triumph over me? (Ps.
>>> 13:1–2)

This doubter was God's chosen king and the hero of Israel. In Mark 9:17–24 we meet another doubter, who asked Jesus to heal his child yet struggled to believe that this was possible. This man "cried out and said with tears, 'Lord, I believe; help my unbelief!'" (v. 24 NKJV). Jesus did not reprimand him or belittle him but answered his prayer and healed the child.

The disciple infamously known as "Doubting Thomas" couldn't believe that Jesus had truly risen from the dead. He declared, "Unless I see the nail marks in his hands and put my finger where the nails were, and put my hand into his side, I will not believe" (John 20:25). Jesus gave him what he needed to believe, saying, "Put your finger here; see my hands. Reach out your hand and put it into my side. Stop doubting and believe" (v. 27). Throughout the Gospels, Jesus addressed the unbelief of his disciples and called out their lack of faith (Matt. 8:26). This does not mean that he gave up on them; he directed rebukes at his most beloved friends—those who would go on to found the church.

Jesus loves doubters. There is room for Jen in God's kingdom. She is wanted.

Most Doubt Is Suffering, Not Sin

Stubborn unbelief—a final decision to turn away from God—is sin. John 3:18 says, "Whoever believes in him is not condemned, but whoever does not believe stands condemned already because they have not believed in the name of God's one and only Son." Doubt, however, is not stubborn unbelief. It is the distressing experience of uncertainty or spiritual disassociation. As discussed earlier, it may arise from unanswered questions, traumatic experiences, or disillusionment. The heart is deceitful (Jer. 17:9), and if we listen only to the siren song of our doubts, we may endanger ourselves spiritually. But doubt itself is not sinful. It is often better understood as suffering.

All human suffering is a result of a malfunctioning creation whose relationship with the Creator is strained (Gen. 3). None of us experience God as we long to, because our experience is warped by sin. Although Christ has conquered sin and promised reconciliation, we still wait for the day when we experience the consuming love of his rule and reign (Rom. 8:19–23). Our doubt is keenly painful because it speaks to our unfulfilled desires. We long to know God and feel safe in his loving presence. When we don't, we have a sense that something has gone wrong. We doubt because we long for God. This is a right and beautiful desire. We should honor the grief of doubt and should treat doubters like Jen gently, because they experience acute spiritual suffering that may be no fault of their own.

Doubt may be shadowed by sin and suffering, but it is also a perfectly natural manifestation of human limitations. Jen is struggling to comprehend an incomprehensible God. This should come as no surprise. God is not like us. He has graciously revealed himself to us, sufficiently but partially, as if "through a glass, darkly" (1 Cor. 13:12 KJV). God's actions in the world are informed by his omniscience, omnipotence, and omnipresence. Our understanding of God's actions is shaped by our very limited human experience. Uncertainty and questions are inevitable. Human minds cannot make perfect sense of things, so we doubt. Perfect intellectual confidence cannot be a prerequisite for faith—otherwise no one would qualify. Jen's doubts may be morally neutral—simply a sign of her God-given human limitations.

God's People Will Always Be God's People

According to the Bible, God chooses us, not the other way around (Eph. 1:11). Saving faith is a gift from God to his chosen people. Ephesians 2:8–9 says, "For it is by grace you have been saved, through faith—and this is not from yourselves, it is the gift of God—not by works, so that no one can boast." God is determined to hold on to those who are his. He has "given" us to Jesus (John 17:24), and Jesus promises to keep us: "I give them eternal life, and they shall never perish; no one will snatch them out of my hand" (John 10:28).

From the very beginning, God has pursued his people relentlessly. He never gave up on Israel, despite its many failings (Hos. 11). Even greater is his determination to preserve the church. Revelation 7:4 uses the symbolic number 144,000 to convey the idea that every single one of God's chosen people will be welcomed into the New Creation—not one will be lost. He will not give up on Jen. You can encourage her with the same words Paul used to encourage the church in Philippi: "He who began a good work in you will carry it on to completion until the day of Christ Jesus" (Phil. 1:6).

Doubters Are Welcome

The invitation of the gospel is still open to Jen and always will be. Jesus welcomes the uncertain, confused, distressed, and spiritually dry. The gospel offers rich comfort and wisdom to doubters. It warns us not to blindly follow our deceitful hearts, yet it also assures us that our questions are welcome before the God who knows all things. The gospel welcomes us exactly as we are and offers us hope when we are in the midst of sin and suffering. May Jen hear the gentle call that Jesus extends in Matthew 11:28–30:

> Come to me, all you who are weary and burdened, and I will give you rest. Take my yoke upon you and learn from me, for I am gentle and humble in heart, and you will find rest for your souls. For my yoke is easy and my burden is light.

Certainty is not a prerequisite for a life-giving relationship with Jesus.

What to Do Next

When Jen has finished sharing, acknowledge the privilege she is giving you by inviting you into her journey. Honor her bravery and recognize her suffering. A simple "This must be really hard" can go a long way.

If at all possible, resist looking or sounding anxious. No one likes to be the subject of someone else's worry. Jen will likely be very sensitive to any signs of concern—she probably expects you to react negatively. A friend of mine once said that the most painful part of her deconstruction journey was the way worry broke the intimacy of her friendships. She felt as if she had to walk on eggshells around her Christian friends. Their anxiety for her, although it sprang from love, felt like rejection.* If you meet Jen's confession with a calm embrace, you will help quiet the shame or fear she may be feeling.

Once you have thanked her for sharing with you, reassure Jen that doubt is a normal, if painful, part of the Christian experience. If her definition of faith is "intellectual confidence or certainty," invite her to reconsider. The God of the Bible is big enough to handle even our darkest doubts. Open the Scriptures with her and consider the truths about faith and doubt on pages 7–9 of this booklet.

---

* Ironically, the anxiety of Christian friends may indicate their own lack of belief.

Offer to continue the conversation. Jen might feel that she is at a crisis point and needs to make a decision today, or perhaps she has already made a decision. By remaining calm and curious, you may be able to offer her a slower way forward. Doubt is a part of the journey of faith. Doubts evolve and change and should be met with discernment. Encourage Jen to remain connected to her Christian community and to be appropriately honest with those around her.

If Jen seems receptive, offer to pray with her and ask that the Holy Spirit would provide his gracious gift of faith. But if Jen doesn't feel comfortable praying, don't take offense. You don't need to pray with her in order to pray for her.

After this conversation ends, there is more for you to do. Your specific approach will be shaped by what you have learned about Jen's heart and story (see pages 9–19), but there are also some more general steps you can take.

Take the Initiative to Check In on Her

Follow up with Jen after your initial conversation. You could offer to meet up regularly with her to discuss her developing thoughts and feelings. If she is resistant to this, continue making an effort to see her when possible. Doubt is a lonely experience, and your persistent friendship may make all the difference. Don't be afraid to ask Jen directly about the things you know she is struggling with. You could give her some apologetic or theological resources that would help answer her particular questions. Even better, you could offer to read and discuss those resources with her. People who are undergoing spiritual suffering or deconstruction often long for a trusted conversation partner.

When I was going through my own season of doubt, I longed for someone to step up beside me as a comrade and a gentle mentor. I wanted someone to challenge and care for me. I wanted someone to offer a listening ear without being judgmental or afraid of my questions. I wanted someone to sit next to me in church, squeeze my hand, and not ask why I was crying. This kind of support felt like too much to ask for, and so I never did. I also struggled to acknowledge the efforts of those who did try to fill these roles for me. Jen might be feeling the same way.

It is possible, however, that Jen may actually want space to *not* talk about what she is going through. She might feel pressured by people's knowing looks and constant questions. She might feel exposed. If this is the case, tread lightly. "Following up" with her shouldn't look like an interrogation. It should look like friendship. Offer her your time, your presence, your thoughts on the weather (okay, maybe not the weather, but you know what I'm getting at). Jen may not want to talk about her doubts right now—and perhaps she never will. She should know, however, that you are with her. You see her and are committed to walking alongside her, in conversation or in silence.

Activate Support Networks

Depending on Jen's age and your relationship with her, it may be appropriate for you to flag her situation with someone who is pastorally responsible for her, such as a youth-group or Bible-study leader, a parent, or a church leader. You should get Jen's permission before you do so and should be clear about why you want to share what she has told you. You can offer to speak to the person on her behalf or can support her while she has the conversation herself. Emphasize that she is not "in trouble." Instead, you are activating Jen's covenant community to care for her, as you would no matter how she was suffering.

It may be, however, that no one other than you needs to know about Jen's situation—especially if her struggles are not affecting her participation in Christian community. If this is this case, you need to respect Jen's privacy and the honor she has shown you by making you her sole confidant.

Whatever you and she decide, you must share Jen's sensitive information with others only on a need-to-know basis and with her consent. Gossiping about her is an easy way to tempt Jen to leave the church and never look back.

Christian and biblical counseling may be a helpful support for Jen as well. If your church offers these services, encourage her to make use of them. If not, you could do some research and refer Jen to appropriate counselors in your area. Depending on the circumstances, you or your church family could offer to cover the cost of a few of her counseling sessions. Such a gift would acknowledge the seriousness of what Jen is facing and demonstrate your care in practical terms.

Rethink Her Leadership Roles

If Jen is in a position of church leadership, you might need to have a difficult conversation about what she needs to do to maintain her integrity in this position. This conversation should involve Jen, obviously, but also potentially the person who leads her area of ministry or someone else on her church session or leadership team.

Depending on Jen's convictions and her ministry role, she may be able to continue serving. Doing so might even help her slow down and exercise her faith in a tangible and simple way. I found that serving at church helped me work through my own doubt with perseverance and patience rather than panic.

I did, however, eventually need to change roles in my church. I found the ministry of leadership distressing and difficult to do authentically, so I adopted a behind-the-scenes role for a time. Likewise, Jen might find that serving in a particular role is unhelpful or goes against her conscience. If this happens, help her think of another opportunity for her to serve. In my personal experience, simple, hands-on tasks can be freeing. Setting up morning tea or coffee, cleaning, or being on parking duty doesn't demand a false smile or a weighty theological conversation. Such simple acts of service require only enough faith to say, "I can do this small thing today." As they add up, they encourage strugglers to renew their trust in Jesus and participate more fully in the work of his kingdom.

In some cases, however, people who are struggling with doubt may need to step down from leadership or service entirely. A few years ago, the assistant pastor of my church experienced a crisis of faith. After praying and persevering in his role for two years, he chose to resign from church leadership and pursue another career entirely. He uses the metaphor of a broken bone to describe his experience. Ministry was putting pressure on the break, and he needed to step away so that it could heal. He did this not to escape the Christian faith but to safeguard his own spiritual health—and the health of the church. His choice was an admirable one. It reflected his confidence that, in his own words, "the Lord walks with his people in the valley." Jen might be in a position of leadership that is impossible or inappropriate for her to continue. A decision to end or pause her role should be made slowly, in counsel with the leadership of the church.*

---

* Special circumstances may necessitate a public announcement to the church community. For example, greater transparency may be called for if Jen is a paid or visible leader in the church.

Help Her Stay in Church

We do not want Jen to leave her church family. This would not be a happy ending to her story. Belonging to a family of believers is a serious commitment and a precious blessing, especially in times of doubt and distress. Your first aim should be to help Jen remain in her church.

Sometimes this will not be possible. You cannot make Jen stay—despite all your support, she may choose to leave her church. Perhaps she wants to find a new Christian community—one that she feels will hold more space for her questions or doubts. She may even have good, albeit tragic, reasons for leaving. Perhaps her current church has serious theological issues or its leadership is guilty of irreparable moral failures.

If Jen decides she must leave her current church, it will be better for her to join a new one—sooner rather than later. Offer to help her find a church she can call home. Be humble enough to step outside your comfort zone as you search, trusting that God works outside your denominational bubble. Of course, you should guide Jen toward a church that preaches the Bible faithfully, but beyond this, any opinions you might have should come second to your desire for her to find a "flock" in which she can receive God's Word and be received and supported by the people around her.

If Jen decides to step back entirely from Christian community, your role in her life will become even more important. Your faithful friendship can demonstrate the loyal love of God. You can gently invite her back to church, but don't do this at the expense of your relationship. Be patient, prayerful, and present in her life. You can't be her spiritual mentor if she doesn't want you to be. You can't change her mind or her life, but you can be her friend. Don't underestimate the influence of real friendship over months and years. Jesus was called a friend of sinners (Matt. 11:19)—he hasn't given up on Jen, and neither should you.

Pray

I hope you can find gentle ways to practically support Jen during this time of emotional and spiritual upheaval. Whatever actions you take, endeavor to be a prayerful and non-anxious presence in her life. Pray daily for Jen's faith. Petition God to enliven her sense of his Spirit and her trust in his Son. When I consider my own faith, which has felt very feeble at times, I am sure that God has been delighted to answer those who prayed for me. Whatever you do, and whenever you're not sure what else you can do, pray for Jen.

Anecdotally, doubters leave Christian community when their questions and feelings are silenced or condemned. Whoever your "Jen" is, she is granting you a great privilege and responsibility by inviting you to speak into her experience of doubt.

In some ways, she isn't actually asking much of you. All you need to do, really, is to listen to her attentively, be a faithful friend, and pray. This booklet has explored some guiding principles that can help you do these things wisely.

Different people experience doubt in different ways and for different reasons, so we've seen that it is worth asking questions to carefully discern the root of your friend's doubt. On the one hand, if her doubt stems from suffering, you're unlikely to help by laying out the cosmological argument for God's existence. On the other hand, she might simply be hungry for answers. At the end of the day, doubt grows from the heart, even if it lives in the mind. Love and gentleness matter, and your way forward must be informed by understanding. Love means listening.

Whatever you do, both you and your friend need to build on sound theology. Our understanding of faith is often narrow and reductionistic in comparison to the complex picture painted by the biblical authors. The complexity of faith is good news for doubters. As you and your friend examine your definitions of faith, you'll see that faith leaves room for questions and lament, for profound emotional experiences and times of spiritual drought. Faith involves a whole person and takes up the span of a life. As you walk alongside your friend, ensure that your understanding of faith is informed by Scripture and is big enough to hold her experiences. And, ultimately, trust that the God she doubts is strong enough to hold her.

In most circumstances, this is not a problem you can or should handle alone. For your own sake and the sake of your friend, call on support networks to rally around her. As you walk alongside her, go gently, holding out the hope of a salvation that does not rest on the strength of a person's faith but on the strength of the Savior.

Tips for Encouraging Communication

Kristina Michael

Sit at the same level as your friend as you converse. Sitting communicates that you are not in a rush; standing suggests that you are ready to move on to the next thing.

Eliminate as many outside distractions as possible. Silence your phone, ensure that someone else is watching any small children, avoid loud spaces.

Ensure you are talking in a safe space that protects her privacy, if appropriate. For example, depending on the type and depth of your conversation, a church foyer—where anyone could walk by and overhear—may not be the best choice of location.

Use body language to communicate that you are ready and eager to listen. Sit comfortably, avoid crossing your arms, lean slightly forward, and make eye contact.

Remember that pauses in the conversation, even if they feel awkward, are OK. Quiet moments allow your friend to process her thoughts and give you time to think about your next response or question.

Mirror her language to encourage conversation. For example, if you ask your friend how she is, and she responds, "I don't know," repeat back to her, ". . . Don't know?" This encourages her to process and to explain more fully what she means.*

---

* For more on mirroring, see Jefferson Fisher (@jefferson _fisher) and Chris Voss (@thefbinegotiator), "How to Get Someone to Open Up in a Conversation," Instagram, August 28, 2024, https://www.instagram.com/reel/C_OjwX-vMdG/?igsh=Zm N5NTdpZTBnZjcw.

Heart Talks Series

WHAT TO SAY WHEN

She Feels Like a Failure as a Mom
Sara Wallace

She's Not Sure She Believes in God Anymore
Brianna Reeves